My Life Around Me

Liliana Palladino

Presentation by *BookLeaf Publishing*

Web: www.bookleafpub.com

E-mail: info@bookleafpub.com

ISBN: 9789357440974

First edition 2023

My Big Sister

I have a big sister called Bella
And she love's eating Nutella,
She loves to do arts and crafts
And especially loves giggles and laughs, it fills
her with enormous glee and even makes her
want to wee but still I love her.

My Favourite Things

These are a few of my favourite things,
I love to wear jewellery especially rings
I love to play games in the day, I love to bake on
Saturday and put the cakes on the tray, I do a lot
of reading and in spelling I'm always succeeding
. THE END

My Favourite Toys

There are so many of my favourite toys!!!!
All of them give me lots of joy!!!
From dollies, to teddies, Lego and cars,
It's really difficult to pick out a star.
The most important thing is to have lots of fun,
Which means that I don't need to choose just
one.

The Shining Rainbow

I love all the colours of the rainbow!
There so bright and colourful.
Red is like fire,
Orange is sweet,
Yellow is like the raising sun,
Green is like the pretty leaves,
Blue is like the sky above us,
Purple is like the delicious grapes and
Pink is like the wonderful tropical flowers.

The Wonderful Nature

In Spring the flowers bloom,
the sun is shining and there is no sign of gloom.

In Summer its so much fun because
you get to spend time with friends
and family. Do whatever you want really.

In Autumn the leaves change colour and
fall of the trees, while days get colder and
shorter.

In Winter Christmas time is coming up,
you get to see your family lots,
you have lots of fun.

My Feelings

In Spring I feel joyful
for all the new life
that is born.

In Summer I feel excited
to go on holiday and
see my family.

In Autumn I feel warm
and cosy , my heart
 is more happy than ever.

In Winter I feel loved and
cared from all those around me,
my body begins to glow because
I also love them.

My Birthday

I woke up one morning to see that it was a
special day just for me, I hopped out of bed and
jumped for joy, I get lots of presents including
toys, I cant wait for my party to start so I giggle
and laugh, we are going to sing a special song
and celebrate all day long.

The Magic Of Christmas

Christmas time is full of magic,
I wish it lasted all year long,
nothing seems to go tragic
and everyone sings Christmas songs,
we get to spend time with family
and have lots and lots of fun,
with children playing lots of
games and quizzes being done,
on Christmas eve we put out
cookies and milk hoping that he will come,
we wake up early to look under the tree
to see if we have won.

My favourite season

My favourite season is Winter because
sometimes it snows!
I like Winter because that's my birthday season.
I like Winter because Christmas and the new
year are in one of the Winter months.
I like winter because I have a lot of fun.
I like winter because I get to see lots of family.

My family

My family mean the world to me
I love them more than your eyes can see
there's Daddy, Mummy, My sister and me,
oh no I almost forgot, our pet dog, Harry
we play, we laugh we joke together
my only wish is that it lasts forever.

my dog Harry

I have a dog called Harry,
he likes to bark a lot,
he pretends to be really scary
but the truth is, he's not,
that's because he's really small,
but he's only trying to protect us all,
but that's why we love him.

my trip to Disney World

going to Disney world was an amazing
experience,
all the rides, the characters and the pool,
it was amazing fun for all,
it made me feel special and excited
because of all the amazing sights,
the villa was amazing and the lights were so
bright .
I really want to go again
but sadly we cant go yet.

my lucky number

my lucky number is 13,
the day that I was born,
some people consider it unlucky,
but for me its a number I adore,
my family call me very lucky
because for me that's the most luckiest number
of all.

my favourite foods

here are a couple of my favourite foods,
I love biscuits and crisps,
I know your probably not going to like this
but I like my vegies,
I also absolutely love pancakes because
the taste is so nice,
those are a couple of my favourite foods
but that's not all there's still more.

my hobbies

I have a lot of hobbies,
like reading, playing, scooting and watching,
those area couple of my favourite hobbies,
if you want to hear more than just ask me.

water

water is my favourite drink,
I usually get it from the sink,
I use it in my showers,
I use it in my tea,
I use it when I have a bath,
its so important to me,
I jump in it when I'm by the pool'
it keeps me nice and cool,
the love of water that I have is so special to me ,
water is free.

my dreams and wishes

I have so many dreams and wishes,
its so hard to explain,
there are so many I'll only tell you some,
so lets start with,
going to ninja warrior again,
going for a toy shopping spree,
having loads and loads of fun with my family,
get more Nintendo switches,
 to be happy and
 to have an amazing life,
those are a couple of my dreams an wishes,
there's loads more but I cant tell you all.

When I get older...

when I get older,
I want to be a teacher or an interior designer,
my mums an interior designer and I want to be
just like her,
but I want to be a teacher because I wanted to be
one my whole life,
I just wish that I could be both.

www.ingramcontent.com/pod-product-compliance
Lightning Source LLC
LaVergne TN
LVHW050313200726
843509LV00015B/3298

This book is about the world around me, my feelings and every day passions

ABOUT THE AUTHOR

Liliana Maria Palladino was born in Epsom, United Kingdom in January 2015.
She has a passion for reading and writing and loves to share her daily thoughts , loves and aspirations through her poetry.

www.bookleafpub.in

Individualism
NATASHA NAND